"This light-hearted story shows how paying atte͟҉͟͟͟ mental and emotional health is one of t͟͟͟ ower and potential. This is a fu ͟͟͟ ghly recommended."

-Ke ͟͟͟ ɔr of *The One Minute* ͟͟͟ ᴜᴇr and *Leading at a Higher Level*

"Amazingly, Dr. Mullen has captured the essence of so much of the tension within today's dysfunctional corporate environment. He helps his readers navigate their path past familiar warning signs to a successful conclusion for both themselves and their employers. A must read for anyone feeling confusion or stress in the workplace."

David Breukelman, MBA
President, Business Arts Inc. & Founder of Arius3D Inc.

"Dr. Grant Mullen addresses in a fresh, non-threatening way, a serious problem affecting many people in business and other walks of life. Recognition that this is a problem that is widespread and for which help is available is a necessary first step to dealing with it. The many examples of the associated dysfunctional behaviour portrayed at Crystal-Display should strike a familiar chord with many readers. Managers and supervisors at all levels should read this book. It's a real eye-opener."

Jacques Lapointe
Retired President and CEO of GlaxoSmithKline Canada.

"I highly recommend this book to any individual or organization that is seeking a workable approach to the creation of balanced and creative management concepts. *The Breakthrough Solution* is a clear, readable presentation of 'the formula to create leadership and an environment that supports it.' It discusses the emotional baggage we all carry that prevents us from reaching our potential and how to deal with it. A great tool for the marketplace."

Ralph A. Beisner
Retired New York State Supreme Court Justice and Author

the

BREAKTHROUGH
SOLUTION

the

BREAKTHROUGH
SOLUTION

GRANT MULLEN M.D.

Release the Potential in People

TATE PUBLISHING & Enterprises

Published by Tate Publishing & Enterprises, LLC
127 E. Trade Center Terrace | Mustang, Oklahoma 73064 USA
1.888.361.9473 | www.tatepublishing.com

Tate Publishing is committed to excellence in the publishing industry. The company reflects the philosophy established by the founders, based on Psalm 68:11,
"The Lord gave the word and great was the company of those who published it."

Book design copyright © 2008 by Tate Publishing, LLC. All rights reserved.
Cover design by Lindsay B. Behrens
Interior design by Nathan Harmony

Published in the United States of America

ISBN: 978-1-60462-715-2
1. Business: Management   2. Office Management/Workplace Culture
08.01.21

Acknowledgements

I would like to acknowledge the invaluable contribution of my friends and associates who reviewed the manuscript and gave me great ideas of things to include and remove.

Daina Doucet, my personal editor, taught me years ago to "Write like you talk and not like a doctor." Throughout this project she had to keep reminding me that "Grammar has rules!" She made the story readable.

My wife, Kathy, has been a constant support and inspiration to "Stop talking about the book and write it." She has graciously adjusted to the challenge of being married to someone with more ideas than output.

Preface

What is the biggest problem to manage in any organization with more than two people? What causes endless frustration and requires a great deal of time to resolve?

People problems! Performance issues! How many times have managers scratched their heads thinking, *I can't figure him/her out. Why aren't they performing as well as I know they could?* How often have you asked the same question—even about yourself? The truth is, humans are an organization's greatest asset and worst liability. Motivated people can lift a struggling company to profitability and dysfunctional people can bring a great business to its knees.

We humans are a puzzle. When all the pieces of our psyche are in the right place, we function at peak potential. Healthy emotions always lead to higher productivity, increased creativity, better working relationships, fewer disability days, lower staff turnover, and happier customers.

But when pieces are missing or out of place, then performance, attitude, and relationships suffer. Emotional disorders cause lower productivity, poor relationships, greater absenteeism, higher disability insurance costs, and increased employee turnover. Mental health conditions are the primary and secondary diagnoses in sixty percent of disability insurance claims. Six percent of all employees have a mood disorder.

Human resource problems of this nature can cost corporations billions. Can we reduce these problems even slightly, save companies millions of dollars, and improve people's lives? The answer is simple! Of course we can—starting with managers who can help struggling people realize their full potential.

The Breakthrough Solution gives you tools not only to recognize and understand the human puzzle, but to take active steps in realizing your own potential and that of your staff.

The Breakthrough Solution reveals the cause of many productivity, attitude, and relationship problems that exist in every organization. It demonstrates an innovative and inexpensive way to unlock potential even in your most difficult employees.

Written in an easy-to-read, light-hearted fiction format, this unique instructional manual tells a humorous story about Crystal-Display—a high-tech manufacturer of leading-edge LCD monitors. Instead of seeing profits soar, the company is on the brink of insolvency. Through the eyes of Bill Spencer, a corporate trouble shooter, you will explore the inner workings of a totally dysfunctional organization. When Spencer eventually discovers a department that leads the company in productivity and performance, he investigates and uncovers the reasons.

Whether you are a manager, supervisor, department head

or an individual who wants to improve your own productivity, profitability, and quality of life, I am convinced you will find this book helpful. Suitable as a guide for group or individual study, *The Breakthrough Solution* can stimulate discussion and corrective action in any department that wants to become an emotionally healthy workplace and reach its peak potential.

Why am I so certain that this book holds answers to many workplace problems?

The Breakthrough Solution was born out of my twenty-six years as a mental health physician. In my counseling practice I saw thousands of dysfunctional individuals and families, and it led me to observe that people always take their personal problems to work. If they struggle with bad attitudes, depression, addictions, and bad relationships at home, they do so at work. Unhealthy dynamics from home are reproduced on a much grander scale in corporations. The workplace becomes a large dysfunctional family as people bring their personal emotional baggage with them.

My greatest satisfaction as a physician has been my ability to help people recognize and correct their emotional problems. As they recover, their performance and productivity at work improves. *The Breakthrough Solution* illustrates both the emotional handicaps that destroy organizations and the significant benefits businesses experience when they correct these problems. Let me encourage you to discover along with Bill Spencer how courageous leadership and a revolutionary management style can release the potential in employees and create a highly productive working environment.

Grant Mullen M.D.

Trouble at Crystal-Display

"What's going on at Crystal-Display?" barked Mr. B., the CEO of Globalcorp Holdings to the assembled senior executives.

They had been reviewing the performance numbers of each of the subsidiary companies in the Globalcorp conglomerate and Crystal-Display, producer of leading-edge LCD monitors, stood out due to its appalling results.

"These numbers don't make sense!" Mr. B. bellowed as he pounded his fist on the report. "How can we be losing market share on the Crystal-Display line? Customer focus groups loved the design of that product! Our distribution channels are excellent. They all want our lighter, compact packaging. We are miles ahead of the competition in our patented processing technologies for this stuff. Sales should be skyrocketing! We should be making a fortune on this product!

"Maxwell," Mr. B. targeted Len. "You've been the vice president of that division for two months. I need an explanation!" Everyone around the table turned to glare at him.

Len Maxwell, newly appointed vice president of Globalcorp's Crystal-Display division, was experiencing his first quarterly review meeting as a member of the senior executive group.

He had seen the declining sales and performance numbers. They weren't the only negative indicators. The Crystal-Display plant was a train wreck. Product defects, manufacturing down times and shipment delays were all on the rise. Absenteeism was the highest in the Global Group of companies. Len had phoned Bruce Sommers, the president of Crystal-Display, to ask about the disturbing results. "No problem, Len, we have the situation totally under control, don't worry about a thing," was Bruce's reply. Len was even more unsettled with that response.

"I don't have all the answers yet," Len stalled for time. "But I'm working on it and I'm sure we'll be able to turn it around," he stated with a false confidence that barely concealed his inner anxiety.

"Good," huffed Mr. B. "Fix it fast! We can't afford to keep losing money on that plant. We'll cut the whole division if we have to."

Len felt his muscles tense and his palms sweat as the cold reality set in that for the first time in his short executive career, his neck was really on the line. He could already feel the daggers from the other vice presidents who knew that a poorly performing division would hold down the Globalcorp share price and the value of their stock options and bonuses. After all the years that he longed to be invited to the boardroom, now he couldn't wait to get out.

Len knew he needed more experienced help to save Crystal-Display and his own neck from the axe. He was able to arrange an emergency meeting that same afternoon with Bill Spencer, the very experienced but low profile management troubleshooter for Globalcorp. Bill had a strong reputation for diagnosing and making key recommendations to turn around struggling divisions.

Len loosened his tie and shifted in his chair. "Bill," he started, "I have a big problem and I'm hoping you can help me." Before Bill could do much more than nod, words pent up in his mind since the board meeting burst forth. "Crystal-Display is floundering. I have to find out why and turn it around or that division and my head will be severed from Globalcorp."

Len's panic was obvious. Bill calmly leaned back in his chair. While his eyes conveyed understanding, he restrained a slight grin, but Len didn't notice. Bill had seen desperation in young, inexperienced executives many times before when they faced their first big test.

"So what do the numbers indicate?" Bill queried, his voice relaxed.

"Well to begin with," sputtered Len as he fumbled with papers containing months of performance data, "sales are dropping."

"Is that because demand is declining for their product?"

"Heavens no!" shot back Len. "Demand for liquid crystal displays has never been higher, but they can't fill orders on time and too many of their displays are being returned defective. Major customers are turning to other suppliers who can fill orders faster and with more consistent quality."

"I see," said Bill as he leaned forward with heightened interest, "so there's a production problem?"

"That's only the beginning." Len couldn't contain his exasperation. "They have the highest number of sick days of any employee group in Globalcorp." Not waiting for a response, he continued, "And the staff turnover rate is unbelievable. Apart from senior managers, no one stays more than three years. Half the new hires leave within six months. Can you believe a place like that?"

"So there's a people problem, too?" Bill inserted while Len paused to take a breath.

"Yes, I think all of Crystal-Display is a problem," sighed Len as he slumped into his chair, a picture of defeat. "That's why I need your help. I need you to find out what's going wrong and help me figure out what to do about it."

"Well, that's a pretty tall order," replied Bill as he considered the size of the problem. "Production problems are easy to analyze, but people problems are a different ball game. It's tough to get honest answers from people if they know they are under investigation by Head Office," Bill reasoned.

Len sprang to life. "Exactly!" he exclaimed. "I have an idea to get around that. No one there knows you or your role at Globalcorp since your activities are never publicized. You could have complete access to every department of Crystal-Display by posing as a reporter for the corporation's magazine," Len smiled mischievously as he continued. "You would be researching an article on how Crystal-Display is meeting the needs of high-tech industry in the 21st Century."

Bill raised his eyebrows as he considered this unusual method of investigation. He quickly realized that people would be much more willing to relax, open up and be honest with a reporter pretending to be writing a complimentary story than with someone carrying out an investigation.

"Okay," Bill replied after a moment's reflection. "It's worth a try."

"Excellent," responded Len with a sigh of relief. "I'll let them know you are coming and the *purpose* of your visit." Len stood and shook Bill's hand gratefully. "Good luck! I'll need a lot of it myself right now."

The Front Door

Bill arrived early at Crystal-Display, long before his nine a.m. appointment with the CEO. He looked around the main floor, grabbed a coffee and sat down in the front lobby to watch people arrive.

He immediately noticed something very unusual about the staff members at Crystal-Display. Most were carrying or dragging a bag of some sort. The bags were of all different sizes and shapes. Some were the size of a small backpack, others like a sports equipment bag, others a camping duffle bag and still others were large enough to hold something as big as a motorcycle. The bags were attached to their arms with a band, or chain, leaving their hands free to hold a lunch bag or briefcase. The bags were uninteresting in appearance, and were made of a dull, colorless canvas or vinyl covering. Oddly enough, the presence of the bags went largely unnoticed by each individual and everyone around them.

The scene at the front entry spoke volumes to Bill about Crystal-

Display. As staff members entered either the swinging or revolving doors, they had difficulty cramming the ever-present bags through the doors with them, causing endless frustration. When two staff members approached the doors at the same time, inevitably the bags, and then the people, collided. A constant stream of cursing and rage exploded from the entrance area with torrents of anger, blame, accusation and name calling as employees stormed to their offices. On at least two occasions that morning Bill heard a raging staff member scream something that included, "I'm taking a mental health day!" They then changed direction and headed straight to the Human Resources department.

It was a bizarre scene

It really was a bizarre scene, and Bill made a note to ask someone as soon as it was convenient what the bags were for. But now, noticing the time, he knew he had to get to his first appointment. As he stood and turned to check directions, he nearly stumbled over the bag of someone passing quickly behind him.

"Oh, excuse me," he said as he quickly regained his balance.

"Watch where you're going!" the staff member snapped and collected her keys that had fallen to the floor.

Taken aback by such ill temper, but not wanting to miss an opportunity for investigation, Bill asked, "Can you tell me why nearly everyone here is carrying a bag of some sort?"

"Bag? What bag?" she demanded, and glared at him. "Mind your own business!" With that she stormed off.

What a toxic bunch! Bill thought. He had never seen such a concentration of hostility before. *Wonder what's in those bags? She pretended they don't exist.* He pulled a notebook from his jacket pocket and recorded his observations: *Most employees have bags. The bags get in everyone's way and cause conflict.*

He then proceeded to his meeting with Bruce Sommers, the CEO of Crystal-Display.

I Hate People

Bill arrived to an open office door and walked in.

Noticing him, Bruce Sommers jumped up from behind his desk and in three strides arrived to meet him. Shaking his hand enthusiastically, he exclaimed, "Welcome to Crystal-Display! We're delighted that Globalcorp has finally recognized what a great job we're doing here. I want you to feel free to speak to anyone and go anywhere in the plant to get the information you need for your article."

Bill returned the greeting, but wondered about the CEO's openness to an outside investigation of his troubled company. Sommers, he couldn't help but notice, had a bag attached to one arm as well. It was quite large, but moved easily along the floor.

"That's a ... rather large bag," Bill ventured.

"Pardon me?" asked Sommers, his train of thought evidently disrupted.

"The ... bag on your arm. It's, uh, rather large!" Bill pointed at his left arm.

Sommers appeared bewildered. "Bag? What bag?" He lifted his arm and looked under it.

Bill felt as confused as Sommers looked. *What is it with these people? It's as if they don't know they have bags attached! What do I do now?* he thought, and attempted a quick recovery. "Oh, nothing. I…made a mistake. I thought I saw something stuck to your sleeve—a tag…on your sleeve!" Bill grinned weakly.

"Oh! Ha, ha!" Sommers smiled awkwardly and straightened his jacket. He let the moment pass. Bill made a mental note, *When the CEO doesn't understand the quarterly reports, there is a big problem. And when he doesn't seem to know he has a bag attached to his arm, there's a bigger one. Better wait to ask about bags at a better time.*

Fortunately Bill's new identity as a reporter seemed to be working perfectly. "So tell me," said Bill, now in the reporter's role, "what's the secret to Crystal-Display's success?"

Having anticipated this question, Sommers launched into a grand speech about his own great leadership that was taking the company into the 21st century. As he strutted around the office praising himself, Bill noticed that the bag never interfered with the flow of self-adulation.

He took notes dutifully for a while, and then interrupted, "Do you have any difficulties or challenges?"

"None that we can't easily handle with visionary leadership," Sommers replied with bravado. Suddenly his face grew somber. He quickly sat down in the chair next to Bill, leaned forward and whispered, "Can we talk off the record?"

"Of course," replied Bill feeling a little crowded for personal space. He put down his pen and notebook.

Sommers's eyes narrowed. "The truth is," he hissed, "I hate the people here, especially the vice presidents. They can't follow orders. They all want my job, and I don't trust them."

What was that? Bill thought, stunned by the extraordinary revelation.

But the moment passed as suddenly as it had come. Sommers leaned back. "Do you know what I think the ideal corporate model should be?" he asked, once again on his leadership stage playing to the audience.

"Tell me." Bill collected himself, now fascinated by such a dysfunctional person in a senior leadership position. He picked up his pen and pad again.

"The A.T.M."

"The automated teller machine—like...at a bank?" Bill was incredulous. His pen remained suspended in mid-air.

"Absolutely," affirmed Sommers. He was now on a philosophical roll. "It's perfect. No employees, works twenty-four hours a day, seven days a week, doesn't speak and follows instructions perfectly. It has no opinions, no feelings, is always available, and is easily replaced. Yes—that's my ideal corporation! No humans!"

Sommers stood to his feet looking very proud of himself. Holding his head high, he turned slightly to gaze out the window. He was clearly lost in the vision of how his company would flourish without people. Bill wondered what he would do next.

There was a long pause, as if he had just delivered an award acceptance speech and was waiting for applause. And then he spoke. "Did you know that even accountants agree with me that machines are the best part of a corporation?" he asked. He didn't wait for a reply. "Machines are always listed as an asset, humans are an expense. What more proof do you want? Let's just face it. People are a nuisance, but a necessary evil. We have to put up with them, but only until we have better machines."

Bill Spencer considered the extraordinary corporate vision that had just been laid out before him. He couldn't imagine hearing something like that from a corporate leader of any rank. *No wonder this company is in trouble. This will be a challenge. Who appointed this guy as CEO anyway?* His question quickly answered itself when his eyes fell on the wall-mounted portrait of Bruce Sommers Sr., the founder of Crystal-Display, and of course, Sommers's father.

"Would you like to join us at our 11 a.m. meeting with the vice presidents?" offered Sommers. "It will allow you to report on the creative, visionary decision-making process that guides our company at the highest level. I'm sure the vice presidents would all love to be profiled in the magazine."

That would be interesting. Bill was certainly curious to see the leaders in action.

Leadership by Intimidation

At 11 a.m. Bill positioned himself in a corner of the boardroom where he could easily watch the proceedings. Each of the five V.P.'s arrived on time. All but one glanced at Bill suspiciously and took their seats in a quiet, almost cautious manner. That one came right over to him. With a warm handshake and a broad smile, he said, "Hello, I'm Peter Wilson from Communications. Welcome to Crystal-Display."

There was surprisingly little small talk between the V.P.s, which made Bill think that these three men and two women were not comfortable with each other. The atmosphere was tense and formal. Like most everyone else at Crystal-Display, they carried bags of different sizes that came to rest beside their chairs when they sat down. All of them, except Peter Wilson.

Moments later Bruce Sommers arrived. As he settled into his chair something very peculiar happened. All the vice presidents, except for Peter Wilson, almost in unison placed their bags on the table directly in front of themselves. The bags now served as a barrier that blocked their view of the CEO and hid them from his direct gaze. What made this scene even more incomprehensible was that Sommers sat behind his own bag, which obscured his vision of anyone else in the room.

They are hiding from each other, Bill realized. *I wonder where they learned that team-building strategy?*

They are hiding from each other.

The meeting began with an introduction of Bill Spencer and his reporting role for Globalcorp. A few polite but cold words of welcome came his way.

"So let's get down to business," announced Sommers. "Markham, do you have a solution for the problem with the Mexican client?"

"We're working on it sir," mumbled the vice president from behind his bag. His head was down and he was fidgeting with his pen. "I only learned about the problem two hours ago and didn't know you wanted a report for today's meeting."

"Well I did! Why shouldn't I?" shouted Sommers from behind his own bag. "I expect every vice president to be ready to answer my questions at any time, with no excuses. If that's asking too much then don't take the job!" Markham slumped in his chair, his face red with anger and shame.

The next agenda item was another vice president's presentation on the market viability of a potential new product. The presentation was reasonably clear, but the speaker avoided eye contact, paused cautiously after each point, and was clearly expecting to be attacked. When he finished, he quickly retreated and positioned himself behind his bag.

"I should have done it myself," snorted Sommers with contempt. "If you folks ever expect bonuses or promotions, there will have to be big improvements in your performance."

The emotional temperature dropped to absolute zero. All but one of the vice presidents slumped even further in their seats. Sommers then went on at great lengths to explain his latest idea and what everyone should do to implement it. When he was done, he asked confidently, "Are there any questions or comments?" Of course there was just a cold silence as they looked away, rolled their eyes, or stared at the floor. "Great! See you next week." With that

Sommers concluded the meeting and the V.P.'s cleared out as fast as was humanly possible.

In a few moments Bill was alone with Bruce Sommers.

"So now you've seen what strong visionary leadership looks like," boasted Sommers. "That's the key to our success here at Crystal-Display. I'm sure Mr. B. at Globalcorp would be interested in hearing about me."

"Oh yes," agreed Bill, choosing his words carefully, "he will be very interested to know who's at the heart of the Crystal-Display story."

Sommers turned on his heel and strutted back to his office, seemingly impressed with his own performance. Bill remained alone with his thoughts. He was flabbergasted. *What a demonstration of dysfunctional corporate culture!* He brought out his notebook and summarized what he had observed:

There is no meaningful communication or cooperation between the executives. Their bags block it.

Sommers is arrogant and oblivious to the feelings or worth of others. He gets angry, paranoid, demanding, manipulative, and needs to be in complete control.

The vice presidents are fearful, passive, ashamed, defensive, and need to hide.

No meaningful or creative work gets done when there is continuous tension and emotions are raw.

This is not a corporate leadership team but a feudal lord with his serfs.

Bill noticed the time and was reminded that he had a meeting in thirty minutes with Cynthia Strong, the manager of Human Resources. As he left the boardroom, he literally bumped into Peter Wilson, who was walking in the opposite direction. Peter asked how his research was going and invited him to coffee. What a pleasant guy! Bill thought. He certainly would look forward to that meeting.

You Can Easily be Replaced

A large yellow banner placed prominently over the reception area greeted Bill when he stepped off the elevator into the Human Resources department. "At Crystal-Display we expect top performance," it said. "You can easily be replaced!"

Now there's a strong motivator! Bill thought sarcastically. *Sounds like Bruce Sommers.*

To get to his appointment, Bill had to walk through the department. He took his time to observe people at work. This appeared to be the largest HR department he had ever seen and it was quite out of proportion to the number of employees at Crystal-Display.

Bill noticed a lineup of people in one corner waiting to pick up forms. He assumed they were applicants for employment. When he got closer he recognized some of the people from the front lobby incident that morning and realized they were there to pick up short-term disability forms. *But they're not sick at all,* he noted. *They're the ones who shouted, "I'm going to take a mental health day!" And it looks like they're all carrying larger bags!*

As Bill moved through the department he looked closely at the people in the cubicles. Most staff members had placed their bags on their desks in front of themselves like the vice presidents had done. But that created a problem. The bags were too big for their desks, so there was very little room for a computer, phone, or paper. Clearly they could do very little work because they had to spend much of their time trying to maneuver the bags around on their desks just to answer the phone or type. One could tell from the overflowing in-baskets that the bags were a significant distraction and really reduced productivity. Bill also noted that people were quite unhappy and unfriendly toward each other. He witnessed one staff member shouting and swearing at a coworker. Moments later she stormed from the department, only stopping long enough to pick up a disability form.

At Cynthia Strong's office, Bill greeted her secretary.

"Ms. Strong is expecting you," she said. He pushed open the door. "You may want to keep your head up…" she continued on, but her voice trailed off as he entered the office.

"Oh!" Bill exclaimed as much in surprise as in pain.

"You're supposed to catch it!" Strong cast him an accusing look as she picked up a twelve-inch rubber fish that had just bounced off his chest and landed on the floor.

"Catch it?" Bill quickly tamed the annoyance he felt. "I'm sorry. I wasn't expecting a flying fish."

They could do very little work

"Well, get used to it," Strong snapped as she drew herself to her full five-foot-two height and stomped back to her desk. "At Crystal-Display you need to expect the unexpected." That had become obvious to Bill in spite of his short time visiting the company.

"We believe in having fun at work," she said sternly as she positioned herself behind her enormous desk. An image of a drill sergeant flashed through Bill's mind. "And one of the signs of having fun is throwing and catching fish."

"It is?" asked Bill. "I wasn't aware of that."

"Yes it is," Strong maintained. "I learned it at an HR conference and I read a book[1] about it. We teach this skill to all new employees. Haven't you noticed what a fun place this is?"

"A...fun place!" Bill repeated, not sure what else to say. *How did she arrive at that delusion?* he wondered.

"So tell me about your department," said Bill, settling into a chair facing her overflowing desk. Resuming the reporter's role, he scribbled a note that she too was carrying a bag.

"We have the busiest department in the company."

"Busier even than the production floor?"

"Yes, we hire and train dozens of new staff every week."

"Is that because the company is growing so fast?"

"No, that's how many we need to fill vacancies and sick leaves."

"That's a pretty high turnover rate," reasoned Bill. "What is your average length of service?"

"About two years. After three years most are gone, except in Communications, where there's no turnover at all for some reason."

Communications? That's Peter Wilson's area. "Why is your turnover so high?"

Strong stood, came around her desk, pulled up a chair close to Bill and sat down. She lowered her voice and said, "Can this be off the record?"

"Sure," replied Bill, noticing a pattern develop. He put down his pen.

"Because they're all morons!" Strong snarled, teeth gritted and eyes flashing. She was back on her feet, pacing and gesturing wildly. "They don't follow instructions. They steal from the company. They are too opinionated—always arguing—and," she wheeled around with a look of utter frustration, "they can't catch fish! Besides, it's cheaper for the company to have most people at entry level wages. We also have a large number of people off with depression and stress leave."

"Why is that?"

"I don't really know, but they are probably just weak and can't take the real working world." Strong appeared to be spent. She plopped unceremoniously behind her humungous desk and almost disappeared. "We can usually see the crash coming."

"If you see it coming, do you do anything to prevent them from crashing and having to be off work?"

"No. There's nothing we can do. It's their problem."

"But it really becomes your problem when you have to replace them," Bill countered.

"We actually use their sick leaves to our advantage."

"How can you do that?"

Strong leaned forward and seemed eager to tell him. "It's a great way to get rid of people. While they are off we make their jobs redundant and eliminate the position. When they want to come back we offer them something we are sure they will refuse. When they resign, we replace them with a person at entry level wages. It's a great way to stay within budget."

Bill had heard enough. The hair on the back of his neck bristled and he was livid. *That's vicious and abusive! No wonder this company is failing. They care about their equipment more than their staff.* He stood to his feet abruptly. "Thank you, Ms. Strong. You have been most informative." The interview was over.

Still troubled with Strong's revelations and uncertain how to report these findings, he found a quiet spot in the cafeteria where he could sort his thoughts. He pulled out his notebook and recorded his observations:

The bags are distracting and disruptive, and they decrease productivity.

The bags interfere with working relationships by making people unfriendly, unhappy, and uncooperative.

The bags increase absenteeism since people with bags don't cope well with stress.

Managers with bags are demotivating. They use fear to control people. They don't value others. They don't care enough about people to spot problems like depression and burnout sufficiently early to intervene and prevent disability.

His bottom-line assessment: *Why would anyone work here?*

The One Minute Leader

The next day Bill had an appointment with Max Trimble, the manager of Accounting. Bill had heard from other staff at Crystal-Display that this department moved at glacial speed. It was frustrating and almost impossible, they said, to get a report or a decision in any reasonable time frame. There was some kind of bottleneck in the system that no one outside of Accounting could figure out.

As Bill approached the office door, he noticed a handwritten sign under the name plate: *The One Minute Leader.* Turning to the nearby secretary, Bill pointed at the sign and asked, "What does this mean?"

She rolled her eyes, "Oh, he picked up that slogan from some conference or book. He thinks it increases his productivity. You'll see what I mean—in about a minute."

When Bill entered the office, Max was on the phone. Right away Bill saw the ever-present bag. It was attached to Max's arm and sat on his desk on top of a mountain of papers. "I'll be with you in a minute," Max whispered, covering the phone momentarily and motioning Bill to sit down. Bill sat in the guest chair next to an end table with an excellent selection of cheese and crackers.

"Sure, sure, no problem," Max continued on the phone, "it should only take a minute, I'd be happy to." With that he hung up the phone and began to hunt for a notepad buried somewhere on his desk among the stacks of papers, files, books, and reports. There was no useable space on the desk, nor was there any obvious order or system to the piles of paper. Max became increasingly frantic as his futile search continued. The bag on his desk was getting in the way of everything Max was trying to do.

Finally he found a scrap of paper and scribbled a note about the phone call. Under his breath he muttered, "I'll never be able to have that ready in time."

Max was walking toward a chair near Bill, when he suddenly stopped. He looked particularly anxious. His eyes darted around the room in a desperate search for something.

"Who moved my cheese? Where is it?" Max shouted and pointed to an empty table next to his chair.

"It's right here," answered Bill, motioning toward the cheese tray beside him.

Max inhaled, quickly composed himself and said in a welcoming tone, "I only have a minute, but how can I help you?"

Before Bill could answer, the phone rang and Max told the caller that he would return the call in just a minute. The intercom then crackled with a question from his secretary and he replied again, "I'll get back to you in just a minute."

Bill could see how Max suited the name on the door. "Why

do you call yourself 'The One Minute Leader'?" he asked when he had Max's attention.

"I was at this great conference, based on a book[2] where every task in management was called the 'One Minute' something," Max began. "I realized that to be an effective manager you should not spend more than one minute on any one task. So that's what I've done ever since, and it has revolutionized my productivity."

Bill could see the state of productivity the revolution had wrought from the state of Max's desk and his corporate reputation. Bill shook his head.

Max picked up some cheese and sat down across from Bill. He began nibbling on it. "Successful managers eat lots of cheese, you know," Max said with his mouth full.

"They do?" Bill took it as a joke, but coughed to suppress a laugh when he realized that Max was serious.

"Yes, I learned it from a little book.[3] Cheese helps you cope with change, so you need lots of it in management."

Bill slid the cheese tray slightly to put down his coffee cup.

"Don't move the cheese!" shouted Max suddenly with pronounced alarm.

Bill startled, rattled his coffee cup, and dropped his note pad.

Not even noticing, Max railed, "Good managers need to know where their cheese is at all times!"

Bill felt like Alice in corporate Wonderland. He had no response to this new revelation, so he chose to redirect the interview. "What is the mission of the Accounting department at Crystal-Display?" he asked, hoping to learn more about Max with a broad question.

At this Max brightened and stood up. Pacing the room, he launched into a glowing description of his departmental mission.

"Accounting is likely the highest evolutionary ability of man, since it brings order out of chaos. As credits equal debits, an individual, corporation, or nation can come into focus and balance to take on the new challenges of the 21st Century."

Bill was impressed that this department was now assisting all of humanity, but when he looked up from his notepad, he suddenly realized what Max was doing as he was speaking. While he was expounding on the glories of balance sheets, Max was using an alcohol-filled cotton swab to disinfect the doorknob, phone, light switches and anything Bill or others might have touched.

Clearing his throat, Bill asked, "Uh ... what procedure is that?" He tried to sound casual, as if disinfecting an office with a cotton swab was normal.

Max was undeterred. "Germs. You can't be too careful. If you're not always on top of them they will soon be on top of you. You never know what comes in the door these days."

Wow! Max is beyond eccentric, thought Bill. *He needs professional help!* Trying again to get the interview back on track, he asked, "Does your staff share your vision of Accounting?"

"Not at all. I can't trust them. They make so many errors, I now have to proofread every report and letter that goes out from this department. Do you see all these piles on my desk? That's what I have to check because of my useless staff."

"Does that slow down the output from Accounting?"

"Only slightly, but I can't be too careful. One slip-up and it'll be my neck on the line, not theirs."

At this point Max sat down again and leaned in close to Bill. Peering at him through thick eyebrows he whispered, "Can I speak to you off the record?"

"Of course," replied Bill, now familiar with this almost predictable component of every interview.

Max glanced nervously from side to side, and then said, "I have to watch my back around here or someone will take my job. Not only that, I can't eat in the cafeteria any longer because it's so germ infested. I'm really worried." Max hung his head and clasped his hands.

"About what?"

"Work, germs, people—everything I guess. I can't get to sleep at night because I have so much to worry about," said Max. He looked defeated as he slumped in his chair.

"Can't you talk to anyone about this? Do you have a counseling program here?"

"Absolutely not!" Alarm crossed his face. "We don't dare go for treatment. If we put in an insurance claim for a mental health drug, Sommers will find out about it from HR. Bruce Sommers said that if anyone needs counseling, then they aren't strong enough to work here. If an executive is off work due to something like stress, anxiety or depression, then his position is made redundant and there's no job to come back to."

"But depression and anxiety are common treatable illnesses. People can make a full recovery." Bill felt angered again at Sommers's HR policies. It was painful to see how they were affecting this manager. "What do people do if they are suffering with depression, stress, or anxiety and they're finding it very hard to work?"

"Just keep going. Look and sound like you're okay. Keep it to yourself." Max looked close to tears.

"But that can lead to suicide!" exclaimed Bill, compassion welling up in him in spite of his detached role.

"Yes, we've had two since I've been here."

An uncomfortable silence met them as each man recognized how much damage this seriously flawed company practice was causing. The interview came to an awkward end.

Bill thanked Max for his time and left to review the information he had gleaned. As he trekked slowly down the hall, lost in the disturbing thoughts of the past few minutes, he heard a friendly greeting from behind.

"Hi, Bill," said Peter Wilson rushing past. "When are we having that coffee? Pick a time and call me."

Bill quickly agreed and Peter disappeared through a doorway. *This guy's not like the others,* Bill thought.

Back at the cafeteria Bill opened his notebook and recorded his thoughts:

Fear causes managers to micromanage, control, and slow down work flow.

When mental health conditions are ignored, not only does productivity suffer, but people may die needlessly.

As Bill closed the book, he thought about Peter again. *Peter Wilson seems relaxed and happy. He has no bag! I have to find out why.*

The Cages

Bill arrived early again for his first appointment of the day to sit and watch how people worked and related to each other. He liked this part of his job. Pretending to be studying some paperwork, he watched office interactions.

Today the customer service representative from the photocopier company was visiting and asking staff members how her products were performing. She was obviously a regular, since people knew her by name.

Within a few minutes a female staff member approached the entrance to the cubicle directly behind Bill's chair. She was invited in by the male occupant. The cubicle walls were just low dividers, and Bill could hear every word.

"I can't take it any longer!" The woman pronounced each word forcefully. She was clearly frustrated and angry. "Brian is impossible to work with and he is ruining our project team. He is rude, arrogant, and never gets his reports completed on time."

"Oh come on now, Pam," replied a male voice in a patronizing drawl. "You've been here two years now, so that makes you the senior member of your team. I'm sure you can handle Brian."

"You aren't listening!" Pam exclaimed. Bill heard desperation in her words. "When I try to direct the team, I'm not getting any support from the managers. How am I supposed to get the project completed on schedule?"

"Just give it some time and I'm sure everything will work out fine." Bill gathered that the man was Pam's supervisor. Suddenly he heard the sound of a phone being dialed. *Did that guy just pick up the phone to dismiss Pam and end the conversation?* Bill wondered.

Pam suddenly burst into tears, sobbing loudly enough for Bill to hear. There was now a crisis in the cubicle. Bill's ears were carefully attuned to how this situation would resolve.

The supervisor slammed the phone down and huffed angrily, "You need to talk to someone, and it's not me!" Bill heard a chair roll. "Sylvia, I need your help." The supervisor's voice sounded from the entrance of the cubicle. "You need to talk to Pam," he commanded, and with that his steps retreated from the scene.

The copier rep? The supervisor had evidently grabbed the first person walking by to bail him out. It happened to be the copier representative! At that moment Bill would have loved to blow his cover and meet the guy face to face. He was furious at the callous disregard the supervisor demonstrated toward the project leader. *The guy didn't even try to resolve the situation. He ignored her and took off! Yet another example of the company's disinterest in their employees. No wonder productivity is so low and turnover is so high.*

Within the cubicle Sylvia's voice, bewildered and sympathetic, cooed questioning and comforting words to a severely distraught Pam.

Bill looked at his watch. He still had time, but he wanted to get out of there. As he left the department he walked by the same supervisor who was now on the phone in a vacant cubicle. "Pam's through here. She doesn't have what it takes. Find me a replacement by next week."

Pathetic! Instead of resolving the situation, they replace the person! Bill fumed. *Disgusting! That's their management strategy? Appalling!* He had much to ponder.

On the way to his next appointment, Bill chose to take a route through an unfamiliar department. Once inside, he noticed what seemed to be a totally different environment than any other at Crystal-Display.

Every cubicle was occupied, and there were at least thirty people in the room. But something seemed amiss. Bill could not hear any voices. No one was talking. No one was even on a phone. All he could hear was the sound of keyboards clicking at breakneck speed.

Bill also observed that in this department each worker's bag was behind their chair rather than on their desk. The way the bags were placed was both an advantage and a disadvantage. Their desks and keyboards were easily accessible, but the entrance to each cubicle was nearly totally blocked. Bill could see only the back of each person's head if they were sitting taller than their bag. The bags created an isolated, enclosed space for each worker and discouraged anyone from approaching.

The bags created an isolated, enclosed space

But now Bill was unsure of his way out of the department. He needed directions. He approached a cubicle, leaned over the obstructing bag and said, "Excuse me," to the busy occupant. There was no response. The worker continued typing and studying his monitor, oblivious to Bill's presence.

Presuming he had not heard, Bill repeated, "Excuse me." This time he gently tapped the person on the shoulder. The worker jumped back in his chair. He pushed his chair against the cubicle wall as if to get as far away from Bill as possible in the confined space.

As the startled and clearly uncomfortable worker eyed him suspiciously, Bill felt as if he had just been dropped into a sci-fi movie scene of a restricted, high security-zone where visitors were unknown.

No longer surprised at strange reactions from employees at

Crystal-Display, Bill decided to press on. He asked for directions to the Marketing department.

The worker glanced around nervously, looking for someone else to deal with this intruder. When there was no way of escaping Bill's request, he stammered, "I ... I'm not sure. I've never been there. Ask someone else." He went back to work and the conversation was over.

There were no signs to indicate what department Bill was in, but he spotted Sally from Public Relations passing through. He had met Sally on his first day during an orientation tour.

"I don't recall visiting this department on the tour," he said when he caught her attention.

"Oh no—we don't want anyone coming through here," she said. Motioning to the enclosed cubicles she whispered, "These creatures don't like people looking into their cages. They avoid all human contact, speak to no one, and only communicate by fax or e-mail. They relate better to machines than humans. We no longer invite them to any company functions and we don't take visitors through here."

"What department is this?" Bill asked, "There are no signs."

Sally's face registered surprise. "Why, Information Technology, of course!"

Bill nodded, and jotted an observation in his notebook as they walked silently past the "cages": *Bags isolate people and block communication.* When they parted, Sally gave him directions.

Disruptive Management

As usual, Bill was early for his appointment. He was to see Sid Green, the manager of Marketing. Again he found a seat with good visibility. He knew marketing people were unique because of their creativity, but what he saw was more on the abnormal side.

Sid Green's office door swung open. He burst into the department and barged into a worker's cubicle without knocking. The worker, startled at first, looked irritated while Sid interrogated her with a barrage of questions. He left as abruptly as he had arrived and targeted another cubicle.

When it was time for Bill's appointment, he entered Sid's office and was greeted warmly.

"Welcome, Bill. You picked the right day to visit."

"Why's that?"

"You'll be able to sit in on a meeting of our creative team and you'll see how we tell the world about the life-changing products at Crystal-Display," answered Sid enthusiastically.

"That should be very interesting," Bill said, but really he wanted to know what Sid was trying to accomplish by disturbing the staff in their cubicles. He chose to take a positive approach. "You have an interesting management style. I was fascinated by the way you interacted with your staff a few minutes ago."

"Yes, you're right. I use a very new management technique that boosts creativity. That's what we need more of in this department."

"But, isn't it a bit disruptive?" Bill tried to downplay the obvious.

"Of course it is!" Sid announced. "That's the whole point. The technique is called *Disruptive Innovation*. I learned it from a book.[4] The author said it can turn entire industries upside down, so I decided to try it."

Not again! Bill looked away and rolled his eyes.

Sid motioned for Bill to join the creative team that was now assembling in the committee room. As everyone took their seats, Bill noted that the mood was more relaxed than at the vice presidents' meeting he attended. Once again everyone had their bags, but they placed them on their laps instead of on the table.

Sid invited each member to present their marketing ideas for the product assigned the previous week. Bill was actually impressed with the quality of research, originality of ideas, and their skill in presenting. He made a mental note: *This team has potential. Finally, a glimmer of hope in this company!*

Each presentation, however, was marred by a recurring theme. Unlike in other departments, where the managers criticized and discredited the ideas of their employees, these people tore apart their own ideas. They commonly ended a presentation with words like "I don't think this will work," or "I'm sure our competitors have already thought of this," or "We'll never get budget approval for this idea." Sid actually tried to be encouraging, but nothing he said could shake their pessimism.

Bill was perplexed. Clearly these were skilled people with good ideas, but they were needlessly criticizing and devaluing their own proposals. They obviously believed lies about themselves and their abilities. The lies crushed their confidence, creativity, and productivity.

After the meeting Bill returned to the cafeteria to record his impressions: *Even talented people here have no self-confidence. The lack of self-confidence torpedoes creativity and productivity.*

I need to visit the assembly line, Bill determined. *I need to see why they ship so many defective products.*

The Zoo

When Bill arrived on the production floor he was stopped, rather than greeted, by Zack Palmer, the supervisor. Zack was a big man with a cap on backwards and a sleeveless T-shirt that revealed his heavily tattooed arms. He had a large bag.

"This is the real world of Crystal-Display," he barked gruffly, loud enough to be heard above the machinery noise. "Without us," he rolled his eyes up toward the corporate offices, "they'd be nothin'. They treat us like slaves—make us work in this pit—then complain that we don't go fast enough. If we caught any of them going through here, we'd lock them up in crates and send them to a landfill. Make this quick. My boys don't like no 'suits' nosing around."

Bill was unprepared for Zack's aggression, and he felt conspicuous in his tie and jacket. It was clear his feet were on hostile ground. "I see," he said somewhat cautiously.

Perhaps Zack thought he saw apprehension in Bill's eyes. As if mellowing, Zack huffed, "I'd better walk you through so you don't get hurt." Bill knew Zack wasn't referring to the risk of an industrial accident.

As they passed each assembly line worker, Zack shouted some derogatory comment laced with an obscenity. The workers responded in kind and when they saw Bill, they added a rude gesture and a curse. Visitors were obviously not welcome in this cauldron of angry, seething humanity.

Each worker was attached to an unusually large bag that was always getting in their way. It clearly slowed them down and caused them to make frequent errors. They were constantly cursing. When two people worked near each other, their bags frequently collided causing both of them to shove and curse until someone separated them.

Bill was particularly interested in seeing the quality control area, since Crystal-Display had such a high return rate for defective displays. *It's one thing to make errors; it's another not to screen them out,* he mused.

There were two men at quality control, one on each side of the conveyor. They both had a clear view of everything that passed by. They seemed to be in an unusually happy, even silly mood, which was incongruous with the rest of the department. They weren't particularly interested in what was on the belt, but they were fascinated with a homemade cigarette they were passing back and forth. It had a distinctive smell that Bill recognized from his college days. As they reached across the belt to pass the smoke, their bags collided with displays passing by, often knocking them over and leaving them cracked. The men took no notice of the defective displays rolling down the belt, or the ones they had damaged themselves.

The men took no notice of the defective displays

"Do you have any problem with quality control?" Bill asked Zack, feigning naivety and pretending not to notice what was going on.

"Nope," Zack shot back arrogantly. "The company gets what it pays for. When they treat us like !@#%&*, then the product will be !@#%&*."

It was a short interview. After a quick thank you to Zack, Bill was grateful to retreat to the cafeteria. *That place is a toxic zoo*, he reflected. *This whole place is toxic!*

He took out his notebook again, and recorded:

Dysfunctional managers at the top create dysfunctional managers all the way down the authority ladder.

Unresolved issues breed resentment and revenge.

Angry people are unproductive and contagious.

Bigger bags are linked to more toxic emotions.

Bags cause conflict, inefficiency, distraction, and product damage.

I can't do much more time here or I'll become just like them, Bill concluded. *I think I have enough information to finish my report. The whole company is unsalvageable. It needs to be sold or closed. The only things functioning here are the pens and pencils. Everything else is a disaster.*

As Bill slumped in his chair with his eyes closed envisioning the coming liquidation, a familiar voice interrupted his thoughts. "So there you are! Do you have time for our coffee now?"

Peter Wilson was cheerful as ever. Bill had descended into such morbid thoughts that he didn't know if he could cope with a pleasant conversation. He also wasn't sure he could look someone in the eye whose unemployment he would soon be recommending. Bill knew, however, that there was something about Peter that he had to uncover—why he was so pleasant and why he didn't have a bag.

"Sure, pull up a chair," Bill sighed as he sat up. Mustering his thoughts with some effort, he attempted to put on the reporter's role once again.

"Just relax, Bill," Peter began. "I know you're not a reporter."

Exposed!

"I beg your pardon?" Astonished, Bill straightened up, realizing that somehow his "cover" had been blown.

"I know you're not a reporter," Peter repeated evenly.

"Who told you that?" Bill demanded. Had someone sabotaged his mission?

"No one," Peter assured him, "It's obvious. You don't ask 'reporter' questions. I know. My brother's a reporter. You talk and ask questions like a management consultant. I can see it in your face. You aren't collecting information for an article. You're trying to figure out what's wrong with this place. Am I right?"

Bill was caught. Should he admit the truth, or should he keep up the reporter's role with someone who can see right through the lie? "Is anyone else suspicious of me?"

"Nope, just me. The other managers never talk to me. They think I'm 'different' and don't fit into the corporate culture here.

They love the idea that you'll make them famous and that they'll attach your article to their resumes."

Bill relaxed. There was no doubt Peter was different. He actually seemed normal. In fact, Peter seemed like the only normal person at Crystal-Display. Perhaps it would be safe to be honest with him since no other managers took him seriously.

"Okay." Bill took a deep breath. "You're right, I can't fool you, so I'll be honest. Globalcorp wants to know what's going on here and why your numbers are so bad." He waited to see Peter's reaction to such potentially disturbing news.

"Yeah, I thought so. I'm not surprised," Peter said. "So, what have you learned? Is there any way I can help?"

Now that was intriguing! Not only did Peter take the presence of a corporate investigator calmly but he volunteered to help. *What's with this guy? He's always in control, nothing threatens him, and he wants to be helpful even though he knows I could close the company.*

"I've learned a great deal," Bill said, "and it's not a pretty picture." Peter nodded knowingly. It didn't appear to be news to him. "Can I ask you a personal question?" Bill added.

"Sure, I'm here to help."

"Where is your bag? Do you keep it in a locker somewhere? Why don't you carry one like everyone else?"

Peter rocked back in his chair and erupted in hearty laughter. Bill didn't quite see the humor. "You're the first person at Crystal-Display to mention the bags. No one dares talk about them here. It's a forbidden subject—at least outside my department. I used to have one," Peter reflected and glanced at Bill, "quite a large one actually. It disrupted my life, thoughts, relationships, work—and it almost killed me. I decided to deal with it and gradually I got rid of it. My life has never been the same since."

Bill considered the information that Peter had just shared. He knew it was important. He sensed that Peter had a key to both the problem and the solution at Crystal-Display. "You know what strikes me as significant?" Bill asked. "I can honestly say you seem like the only normal person I've met here, and you're the only one I see without a bag. I just can't help thinking there's a connection."

"You're right. There's a connection, but there are a lot more people here without a bag than just me. Most of them are in my department. That's why you haven't seen them much around the building. Meet me in my office tomorrow and I'll tell you my story."

Just then Bill's cell rang with a text message from Len Maxwell, "When will your report be ready? We need answers soon!"

Peter's Story

The next day, Bill arrived in a positive frame of mind. He made his way to the Communications department, which included the mail room and customer support call center. He had never been to this part of the building or met any of these people. He took a seat in an open area where he could watch the activity. *So, let's see how a vice president like Peter makes a difference to the working environment,* Bill thought. He was not disappointed.

As soon as he sat down a friendly passerby greeted him and asked if she could bring him a coffee or magazine while he was waiting. As she returned to her desk, Bill made a mental note: *She has no bag. That's interesting!*

Around the department he could see people in friendly animated discussions. There was laughter as someone passed a cubicle and made a comment. Everyone was busy, but a sense of camaraderie prevailed. They seemed to like each other. Posters on the walls announced departmental picnics and sporting events. They were also raising money for a charity of the month. On the walls of many cubicles were small "Gung Ho" stickers.

Just as Peter had said, Bill noted that very few people had bags, and any bags they had were very small. He jotted this observation in his notebook.

"Hi, Bill! Come on in!" It was Peter Wilson. "Welcome to Communications."

As they took their seats Peter's secretary knocked quietly, opened the door, and delivered a tray with coffee mugs and a plate of cookies. Peter thanked her and placed them on the coffee table. Bill noticed how different Peter's office looked compared to those of the other vice presidents and managers. His desk was busy, but tidy. Everything seemed organized and in its place. The walls, blinds, and furniture in earthy tones seemed to accentuate a quiet peacefulness. He saw several "Gung Ho" stickers here, too. "How do you maintain this oasis?" he asked.

Peter laughed. "Fortunately, the rest of the company leaves us alone. This department has the highest productivity, lowest absenteeism, and we are always within budget, so they have no reason to come here and make changes. You might say we have a truce with them."

"What's with the 'Gung Ho' stickers here? I don't see them anywhere else."

"*Gung Ho* is a book by Ken Blanchard. It's the best management manual I've ever read and it has really boosted productivity and morale around here. You should read it and pass it on to Mr. B. at Globalcorp."

Finally someone was making correct use of a management book, Bill noted.

"So what makes you tick, Peter? How come this department is functional? Where is everyone's bag?" Bill didn't waste any time launching into the questions that had been foremost on his mind from the previous day. He knew he was about to find the missing pieces to the Crystal-Display puzzle and he overflowed with questions.

"Okay, slow down," interrupted Peter, waving his arms to block the flow of interrogation. "I'll explain what happened and how we got here. It's a long story.

"Twelve years ago I started at Crystal-Display on the production floor…"

"The production floor! How could you survive there?" In his astonishment Bill barely managed to swallow the coffee he had just sipped. "You're from a different planet than those guys!"

Peter smiled. "It wasn't hard actually. Back then I was no different. I was an angry, pot-smoking alcoholic, so I fit right in. I could brawl and curse with the best of them."

Wow! It's hard to imagine Peter like that. Bill couldn't quite process this.

"I was an irresponsible jerk, wasting all my money on destructive habits."

"What turned you around?"

"My wife left. She couldn't take it any more. I ignored her warnings. I couldn't believe she would actually go." It was clearly a painful memory. He paused for a moment in reflection, hung his head, and stared at the floor.

"I was shattered," Peter resumed. "My life was suddenly empty. I started to hate myself. The pain inside got so great that I drank more and tried to stay continually stoned. I was in so many fights at work that I was suspended for a week.

"To fill time, and to get my mind off reality, I started going to movies every night. I just went to the multiplex and watched the next movie on the line-up without even noticing the title. One night I found myself watching *The Kid,* with Bruce Willis. When I saw Willis I thought to myself, this'll be good, lots of action. But in this movie he didn't shoot anyone, or blow anyone up. It was the story of a very successful but dysfunctional consultant, Willis, who finds a boy in his house that turns out to be himself at age eight. The two of them visit past memories to discover what went wrong in his life, and what destroyed his dreams.

"At the climax of the story the adult and child relive a painful family event and realize that at that time, they had believed a lie about themselves. This lie had shaped the rest of the Willis character's life and resulted in the adult being so dysfunctional. When he realized that the belief was a lie, his personality transformed. His life came together in a beautiful way and his dreams came true. At the conclusion he yells for the whole world to hear, 'I am not a loser!'

"By the end of the movie I was just sobbing. I saw myself in so many parts of the story. I had become totally dysfunctional. Nothing was working in my life. I was in unbearable emotional pain. I was a loser.

"I couldn't leave the theatre. I kept sitting there sobbing. Then I noticed something for the first time in my life. There was a bag on my lap! I had never noticed it before. It was very strange and hard to describe. I pushed it away because I felt foolish holding onto a bag like a security blanket, but I couldn't get rid of it. It was attached to my arm in a way that I couldn't disconnect.

"When I left the theatre, I tried to hide the bag, but for the first time I noticed that most other people had bags too and they took no notice of them. I decided just to pretend it wasn't there and to walk normally. In the car, on the way home, I found myself still thinking about the movie. Each time I started to cry I noticed that the bag had somehow arrived back on my lap and I was holding it again. I'd push it away and think about something else, but whenever I remembered what a loser I had become, the bag was back on my lap."

Suddenly Bill understood. *The bag is somehow connected to pain! And that makes sense!* Thoughts, one after the other, lit up in his mind. *The bigger the bag, the greater the pain! That would explain why the most dysfunctional people carry the largest bags.* "That is incredible," he said. "How did you get rid of it?"

"That night I decided to stop my downward spiral. I had to do something. Nothing magical was going to rescue me. I wasn't a character in the movie. I had to take action myself. I needed to talk to someone, and fast."

"So where did you go? Who did you talk to?"

"First I went to Human Resources at Crystal-Display to see if they had an employee assistance counseling program."

That was a mistake! Bill's thoughts jumped ahead.

"That was a mistake," Peter continued. "When I asked about it, Strong looked at me like I was crazy. 'What would you need that for?' She asked. She just scoffed at me. 'Counseling is only for head cases, we don't need it here.'

"I felt totally humiliated, but I was determined to turn my life around. My wife's company did have a program and they accepted spouses. I immediately made an appointment.

"I was so nervous going to a counselor for the first time. I felt ashamed that I had become a 'head case' and needed 'professional help.' I didn't want to be seen there, or to be recognized, so I kept my head down and avoided eye contact. I cringed when I heard the words, 'Come in, Mr. Wilson.' But once I was in there, I just collapsed on her sofa. My recovery journey had finally begun.

"The counselor immediately put me at ease. She was warm and welcoming. She seemed genuinely interested in what was bothering me, so I poured out the whole story—even the part about the movie. But I didn't say anything about the bag. I was too ashamed to tell her about that." Peter chuckled and glanced at Bill. "As if...!" he said.

Bill smiled. He could tell what was coming.

"'Why are you holding that bag?' she asked me as soon as I finished.

"I was so embarrassed. I hadn't realized that as I was explaining my problems and pain, the bag ended up on my lap again. There was no way I could hide it now. 'I don't know. It always happens when I get upset,' I told her. After that our conversation went something like this." Peter related both parts as if in a skit, shifting the tone of his voice between his voice and the counselor's.

"'Do you think there is some connection between your emotional pain and that bag?'

"'I don't know. You tell me. You're the expert.'

"'Have you ever looked inside it?'

"'No, I never thought of that.'

"'Would you like to?'

"'I'm not sure. I'm sort of afraid to.'

"'Would you be willing to try if we went very slowly and did it together?'

"At that point I agreed—just out of my desperation to get well," Peter explained. "I unzipped it just enough to reach inside. What I found was a real shock.

Each page represented a memory or event from my past

"There were many bundles of letters, photos, handwritten notes, and toys. They were mostly from my childhood. Each page represented a memory or event from my past.

"'Can we read some of the notes?' the counselor asked. She was very gentle.

"I picked up one page and read in my own childish printing a brief description of an event where I had answered a question incorrectly in class. At the bottom I saw in large red letters, '**I AM AN IDIOT.**'

"I picked up another and read my description of a time my father spanked me for something. At the bottom were the same large red letters, '**I CAN'T DO ANYTHING RIGHT. I'M TOTALLY BAD.**'

"Over and over I picked up pages where I had written a description of a painful event in my childhood, and at the bottom of each memory in large red letters were the conclusions I had made about myself. '**I WILL NEVER LEARN. NO ONE WILL EVER LIKE ME. I CAN'T TRUST ANYONE. I AM A LOSER. I WILL NEVER AMOUNT TO ANYTHING. I HATE MYSELF. I'M NOT WORTH ANYTHING. PEOPLE ARE DANGEROUS; TRY TO AVOID THEM.**' It just went on and on. Pages and pages of terrible things I had written about myself.

"The counselor asked me why I had written those things about myself.

"I thought about it a bit. Obviously all those things had happened to me and they had really hurt me. So why would I have written those conclusions about myself? I guessed that every time I was hurt I had wanted to figure out why it had happened.

"The counselor wanted me to keep thinking about it, and asked if I noticed some common themes that ran through each conclusion. Since she mentioned it, I had to say, 'Yeah, I guess I do!' The most common theme was, It's always my fault, and the second one was, Avoid people; they'll just hurt you.

"Then she made me look at my conclusions, and asked, "'What do you think about those conclusions now that you are looking back on the events as an adult?'

"It was obvious I had overreacted as a child and taken an extreme position toward myself and others. There was very little truth to most of the conclusions, but they did indicate how upset and hurt I had been. They had seemed to be the right conclusions at the time when I was hurting.

"The counselor understood. She said, 'You must have really been hurt by those events to believe all those lies about yourself and others. Do you think any of those lies have an effect on you today as an adult?'

"My initial response was, No, of course not! That's all childhood thinking. But then when I stopped to think about it more, I had to ask, why was I at a counselor's office anyway? I was feeling useless, hopeless, a total loser. I didn't want to be with people, I didn't trust anyone, and I was really hurting. My life was at a total standstill. Those red-lettered conclusions described how I was still thinking as an adult!

"It was like a huge ball of light exploded in my head. It was my *eureka* moment. I could see it now. It all made sense. 'I get it!' I finally told her. 'I still believe those same lies today and they are messing me up the same way they did when I was a kid.'

"She smiled in that annoying, what-took-you-so-long kind of way.

"The lies had stayed with me even though I'd long forgotten the events that caused them. 'This bag is full of painful memories and the lies that went with them,' I told her. 'When I get upset it's because the lies in the bag are bothering me. The pain is coming from the bag of memories and lies.'

"The counselor explained that the bag is what many people call *emotional baggage*. 'Do you want to get rid of it?' she asked.

"I almost couldn't believe it was possible. I actually asked her, 'You mean I can?'

"She was great. She said, 'Of course! I'll show you how we can do it together.' She told me to pull out a memory.

"I reached into the bag and pulled out a test I had failed in grade three. At the bottom I'd written, '**YOU ARE STUPID AND WILL NEVER LEARN. YOU CAN'T DO ANYTHING RIGHT.**' The counselor walked me through it.

"'Do you still feel that way about yourself?' she asked.

"I had to admit, well, yes—actually I'd always considered myself to be stupid.

"'Is it *true* though?' She just kept pressing me. 'Have you learned *anything* successfully and done things right?'

"I supposed I had, I told her. I'd done quite well in trade school. My first boss really liked my work. She asked if all these years I'd been believing a lie about myself.

"Again I had to say, yes. I'd always put myself down because of what happened when I was a kid.

"So she asked, 'What should you do with that test result and your conclusion about yourself?'

"I tore it up into tiny pieces and threw it away.

"She basically explained that we could unload my whole bag that way and get rid of all the lies. She said, 'Every time we meet, you can pick something out of the bag and we will determine if your conclusion was a lie. When you realize the truth about that situation you can tear up the memory and the lie.'

"That was my first meeting with her. I was amazed by what had happened. For the first time I felt hope. Over the course of the next year I met with the counselor regularly to unload the bag. We gradually tore up every painful memory and lie. When the bag was empty,

I didn't have to carry it anymore and I was free! What an incredible feeling. It was like getting my life back again, but with a whole new way of thinking.

"People at work noticed how different I had become. I was promoted regularly as supervisors saw my performance and how well I now related to other people. Eventually I even got the courage to call my wife and tell her what happened. Of course, she was skeptical at first, but she agreed at least to meet with me. She was very surprised to see how I had changed and put my life back together. She agreed to go to the counselor with me so we could rebuild our marriage. Through the months of marriage counseling she even slowly got rid of her own bag. We've now been back together for the best three years of our lives.

"It's made a huge difference to be free of the bag and all the lies I believed about myself and others. It's easy to see now how bags mess people up at work, reduce their performance, and interfere with relationships. I decided that one of my top priorities as a V.P. would be to help people get rid of their bags. That's why so few of my team have bags. As people get rid of them, their performance and relationships improve. They become more successful. Successful team members create a more successful department. We have the fewest people with bags and the highest productivity."

Bill was speechless as his mind processed Peter's story. He was utterly captivated by the uniqueness of what he had just heard. Now that he understood the bag and how it affected people, he saw that Crystal-Display was paralyzed by a dysfunctional workforce controlled by lies resident in their own emotional baggage. "Did everyone have to go through the same process you did to get rid of their bags?" Bill asked as his thoughts cleared.

"Not exactly," Peter answered. "We each took a different path, but with the same result, and no one did it alone. You need to talk to some of the others in the department to hear how they did it. I'll arrange for you to meet with two of my supervisors, Ned Barclay and Sylvia Peet."

After the meeting Bill once again returned to the cafeteria and to his notebook. This time he was hopeful, and for the first time he recorded a positive finding.

The bags contain records of past emotional injuries and lies the person believed at the time.

Lies from the past affect behavior, relationships, and productivity today.

A counselor can help the person recognize the hurts of the past, correct the resulting lies, and get rid of the bag.

People without bags perform much better at home and at work.

Bill was now looking forward to what he would learn from Ned and Sylvia to help complete the puzzle of Crystal-Display. That evening when he checked his e-mail he found another anxious note from Len Maxwell pressing him for news and reminding him of the report deadline. At least now he was able to report progress in understanding this unusual place.

Ned's story

The next day Bill was eager to meet with Ned Barclay, one of the supervisors in Communications. Ned arrived soon, greeted Bill with a warm handshake, and ushered him into his office. Like Peter, he too was relaxed, friendly, and confident. Most important, Bill saw that Ned had no bag.

"Peter tells me you've noticed there's something different about our department," Ned laughed, knowing he was stating the obvious. "Do you have any questions I can help answer?"

"I'm amazed that your department can be so pleasant and productive in a corporation like this," Bill said. "How do you do it?"

"Well, Peter is the difference. He transformed this place. His attitude and management style are so different from anyone else I've ever worked for."

Bill couldn't help but agree. "So, how did he turn this department around?"

Ned turned off his phone and settled in to tell a story. "First you need to realize that this department was no different from all the others when Peter came. We were nasty to each other and to the customers. Productivity was terrible and people took so many mental health days that projects couldn't get completed. Staff turnover was high since the new hires couldn't stand the atmosphere."

Bill smiled at Ned's assessment. "That pretty well describes Crystal-Display."

"When Peter became my supervisor, I found him annoying."

"Annoying?" Bill interrupted. "How could Peter be annoying?"

"Well, he was always so pleasant and cheerful," Ned explained. "He was interested in me and asked questions about my work and my life. I couldn't stand it. I really didn't know how to respond. He made me uncomfortable. I later learned Peter had a very different philosophy about work."

"In what respect?" Bill prompted.

"He always said people were the single most important asset in any organization. Depending on how they were treated, he said people could be the greatest strength or greatest weakness in a company. He taught me that great people can turn an average company into an industry leader, and that unhappy, unproductive staff can bring a great company to its knees. Peter was committed to transforming our department into something great by helping each staff member reach their highest potential."

"That sounds like a very difficult assignment in a place like this," Bill reasoned.

"It was, and I hated it. I didn't want to change. I showed up for work, did what I had to, then got out as fast as I could and went to a bar to try and forget about the day. I couldn't care less about *productivity* or *job satisfaction*."

"So how did you ever get turned around?"

"Well, my life wasn't going very well. Things weren't pretty at home. My oldest son was in trouble with the police. My wife despised me because of my drinking, and I couldn't stop. I couldn't face how bad our lives had become.

"One day when I was badly hung over at work, Peter called me into his office. I knew this was it. I was a goner. The only good thing left in my life—the paycheck—would now be gone and I'd be on the street bleeding by the time my wife had finished with me. I slumped into a chair in Peter's office and braced myself for the axe. Then he said something I won't forget."

This was interesting. With the memory of the supervisor's interaction with Pam in the back of his mind, Bill wanted to compare how Peter handled a serious and delicate situation with an employee.

Ned continued. "Peter said, 'Is there anything I can do to help you?'

"I had to give my head a shake. 'I beg your pardon?' I asked. I couldn't believe what I had just heard.

"But Peter was serious, and he said it again. 'Is there anything I can do to help? You don't look too good. I've noticed that your work has been slipping over the past few months. How are things going with you?'

"I didn't know how to respond. No one had ever treated me like that before, especially not a supervisor. I mean, he was kind and respectful. Why would he want to help me? Why not just replace me? 'Aren't you going to fire me?' I asked.

"'No,' he said.

"'Why not?' I asked. I almost wanted to tell him he should!

"And then he said, 'Because you have potential, whether you can see it or not. It's my job as your supervisor to help you reach your full potential. That'll be good for you, for me, for the department and for Crystal-Display. It's faster and cheaper to get you back on your feet than to hire and train a replacement. It's just good business sense to look after the investment the company has already made in you.'

"I was stunned. I had never heard such words about me before. He thought I had potential! He wanted to help me find it! He told me Crystal-Display had an investment in *me*! Even my parents never encouraged me like that. I'd always been treated like a stupid, dead-end troublemaker. This was a new experience for sure.

"I decided to be honest with him, so I flat-out told him, 'I hate my life and I drink to try and forget about it.'

"But Peter was pretty sharp. 'Okay,' he said. 'Let's get started on your drinking first. When you're sober, then we'll work on your life. Have you ever heard of Alcoholics Anonymous?'

"Sure, I'd heard of it. I thought it was only for losers who had nothing else to do but go to meetings. 'Yeah,' I told him, 'and I'm not interested.'

"He wasn't fazed. He handed me all the information on AA groups in the area and said, 'Well then, find yourself a better rehabilitation program and start this week. You have to be in a program by Friday or your job really will be on the line.' He told me to report to him every week until I was back on my feet. He really wanted to work with me. He said, 'Let's work together and get your life turned around.'

"With that, the meeting was over. I walked slowly back to my desk. I had dodged the bullet, but only barely. For the first time I had met someone who believed in me, someone who saw a potential in me that had escaped my own notice. Peter was going to hold me accountable for my own rehabilitation. It felt good and scary at the same time. I knew I had to do it or lose my job, family, and home."

"So, you did it then?" asked Bill.

Ned shrugged and smiled. "I had nowhere else to go, so I read through the AA brochures and made up my mind to try a group meeting. I actually went to one that evening. What a surprise it was."

"Why's that?"

"Well, I was expecting a bunch of losers, but instead I found ten of the nicest strangers I had ever met. They were so warm and welcoming to me that I quickly relaxed. During the meeting they were brutally and refreshingly honest. I had never seen adults be so blunt about their own failures. They shared their stories of alcohol abuse and how it ruined their lives. Then they explained how the twelve steps of AA saved their lives and *restored them to sanity*. These men and women were from a wide range of social strata and occupations but they had one thing in common—a history of alcohol abuse and a commitment to recovery from it. The evening went so well that I felt I had made several new friends and I wanted to go back. I wondered if maybe they really could help me.

"At the next meeting, I learned how to get started by using the twelve steps. Step one was to *Admit that I was powerless over alcohol and that my life had become unmanageable.* That was an easy step to take. I already knew it was true.

"Step two was to believe that a *Higher Spiritual Power greater than myself could restore me to sanity.* Now this was getting harder.

Step three was even worse. It said I had to make a decision to *Turn my will and life over to the care of this Higher Spiritual Power*, however I wanted to define it."

"What made that so difficult?" Bill interrupted.

"It was totally foreign to me. I didn't know anything about Higher Powers. I didn't have any spirituality or a sense of the presence of an unseen force. My family hated religion and blamed God for all the bad things that happened to us. The last time I was in church was to get married. To me reality was what I could experience with my five senses. No more, no less. I was used to looking after myself. I didn't want to be controlled by some invisible myth."

"So, did you quit the program at that point?"

"I wanted to, but I just couldn't get away from the fact that all these new friends had been as messed up as I was and they were now sober and getting on with their lives because of these twelve steps. There had to be something powerful about them. I didn't want to make a mistake by closing my mind to something that could help me even though I didn't understand it. I knew I needed more than willpower to stop drinking—I had tried willpower many times and seen nothing but failure.

"The group assigned me to a sponsor with whom I could meet personally to ask questions. At our first meeting I asked him why spirituality was so important to the AA program. He explained that all humans are spiritual. It's like our moral rudder—our ethical compass and our inner standard of morality and integrity. It's what gives us meaning and purpose and a reason to get up in the morning. It's our sense that our lives are part of a bigger picture and that our actions have significance to mankind. Healthy spirituality gives an inner strength that helps us through good and bad times. It is this strength that helps us conquer alcohol. Without it, you're on your own in a downward spiral.

"I decided that I would take a chance and believe that there was a Higher Power who could help me out of my life's mess. I had nothing to lose. Trying to fix myself didn't work. Besides, I didn't have to become religious or join a church. I just needed to find a relationship with a Higher Power. Once I had overcome the spiritual hurdle, the other steps were much easier to understand and carry out."

"So did it work?" Bill asked.

"It took time, effort, and perseverance for me and my sponsor, but I gradually trained myself to rely on my Higher Power to resist the urge to drink. It's hard to put into words, but I really did feel helped and supported by my Higher Power. To my great surprise, I had become a bit spiritual and it actually felt good. My wife had always gone to church and considered herself to be spiritual, but I had never been interested. Now I was. I began to wonder what the difference was between her spirituality and mine. I decided to go and talk to her pastor.

"He was quite interested to meet me, since he had only heard about me from my wife. I'm sure he had never heard anything good. He seemed like quite a decent person, so I explained to him my spiritual journey and beliefs. I then asked if there were any similarities to his beliefs. He actually told me that my Higher Power had the same attributes as his God, and that my wife and I now had a very similar and compatible spirituality. Having settled that question in my mind, I decided to swallow my pride and begin going to church with my wife. I hoped to try and increase our common interests and strengthen our shaky relationship. She of course was stunned and skeptical at first. She gradually got used to me coming with her as she saw how committed I was to sobriety and to an active, daily spiritual life."

"Wow, that was a major turning point in your life," concluded Bill.

"Absolutely, you just can't overstate the fact that AA saved my life, my marriage and brought my spirit to life."

"How did your weekly meetings with Peter go?"

"He was delighted and encouraged me every week to stay in the program. He did everything possible to help me through the rough times when I didn't know if I was going to make it. Between Peter, my sponsor, the group, and my Higher Power, I was carried to sobriety and a new life.

"After about six months of sobriety, Peter dropped the second shoe on me. I thought I had been doing really well, but Peter had bigger plans. During one of our weekly meetings Peter said, 'Do you notice what you are carrying?'

"'No,' I told him. 'I don't see anything.'

"'Do you see that bag attached to your wrist?'

"For the first time I became aware that I was carrying a large bag that I couldn't detach from myself. 'Okay, yeah,' I said. 'I see it. What is it?'

"'That's a long story,' he told me, 'but trust me, you don't want to carry it around for the rest of your life. That bag is holding you back from success in your work and personal life. It likely was part of the reason for your drinking problem.'

"*Wow*, I thought to myself. *Does Peter know everything?* For the first time I noticed how many other people in the department were carrying bags, but Peter wasn't. The next time I talked to him, I asked him, 'Did you ever have one?'

"'Sure did,' he said. 'A very big one.'

"'How did you get rid of it?' I wanted to know.

"'I had to see a specialist in baggage,' he told me. 'It changed my life when I got rid of it. Here is her name.' He gave me her phone number and told me to go see her and get rid of the bag.

"So, I did what he suggested and she gave me the same treatment. I soon realized that all the painful memories from my childhood were in the bag. The memories had caused me to believe lies about myself that were disrupting my adult life. The counselor helped me understand that I drank to dull the pain coming from all the bad memories in the bag. Over several months we emptied the bag and corrected all the lies that I had believed about myself.

"The bag was now gone and I felt so much better. My marriage had been restored, since I was now a much easier person to live with. My work was going better because I could concentrate, be productive, and creative. I was even getting along with my coworkers."

"How did Peter think you were doing?" asked Bill.

"A few months later at my weekly meeting with Peter, he congratulated me for my progress over the past year, and that I was now one of the few in the department who no longer carried a bag. He had also noticed how well I was getting along with other members of the department. Then he said the unthinkable to me.

"'I want to make you a supervisor.'

"I didn't know how to respond. I never expected that!

"'You're a different person from the Ned I knew one year ago,' he said. 'You've conquered your habits, gotten rid of your bag, and you are now demonstrating leadership abilities in your work. You are exactly the kind of person I want for our leadership team.'

"Then he explained his leadership philosophy to me. 'On this team,' he said, 'we lead by example. When we have dealt with our own issues and released our bags, we are ready to lead others. When a supervisor has not dealt with their own issues, it can hold back the entire department from achieving their potential.' He told me I now qualified for leadership. 'How about becoming a supervisor?' he asked.

"I felt pretty stunned. I had never been promoted before. I never thought I had the potential to rise in any workplace. But then I remembered that one of the lies I had torn up with the counselor was that I would never succeed. Since that lie was now destroyed, I figured, I was free to accept the promotion. So I did!

"Peter welcomed me to the management team with a handshake and a slap on the back.

"So here I am today, a supervisor, making more money and having more fun at work and at home than I had ever dreamed. I owe it all to Peter. He cared about me, believed in me, and pointed me in the right direction for recovery. I'll follow him anywhere. Now I do the same thing with the people who work for me. I'm seeing two of my employees every week while they go through a recovery process. We keep the counselor busy."

"That's an incredible story," Bill said shaking his head. Through the office window he could see that people were tidying their cubicles and drifting toward the door. It was almost time to leave. "I can see how Peter's attitude has become contagious," he added, and chatted for a few more minutes with Ned before gathering his things and heading back to the hotel. "Thanks so much for sharing your story with me," he said to Ned on parting. "It has given me a lot of insight."

That evening Bill summarized the day's findings in his notebook.

Those who are free of bags want to help others find the same freedom.

Those who are free of bags make excellent leaders.

Healthy spirituality gives people meaning in life and the strength to overcome adversity.

Sylvia's story

Bill returned to the Communications department the next day and sat in his usual chair waiting for Sylvia Peet. Several staff walked by and greeted him like an old friend. They were getting accustomed to Bill's presence in the department.

Bill thoroughly enjoyed it. *That's amazing,* he marveled. His thoughts tumbled over one another. *In the other departments I was an unwelcome intruder, but here I'm a friend and colleague. What a unique working environment! I wonder what Crystal-Display would look like if Peter's management ideas were used in every department?*

His happy reverie was interrupted with the arrival of Sylvia Peet.

"Good afternoon Bill," she said with a wide smile and a firm handshake. "Come into my office and have a coffee."

While she was pouring, Sylvia began, "Peter tells me you are doing an article on Crystal-Display for the company magazine."

Bill looked up, startled, not knowing which role to take for this interview.

Sylvia winked and smiled at him playfully, so Bill relaxed. "It's about time someone from Head Office came here to see what's really going on in this company. They also need to see what Peter is doing in this department to turn things around."

"I can assure you," Bill answered, "Head Office will soon know all about the internal dynamics of Crystal-Display."

"If it wasn't for Peter's courage to stand his ground and stick to his principles," Sylvia continued, "we would still be absorbed by the corporate chaos beyond our department doors."

"You are very fortunate to have a V.P. like Peter," Bill summarized.

"I'll say. You know he saved my life."

"Really?"

"Yes, he saved my life … literally."

"Literally?" *Unless Peter had pushed her out of the path of a speeding delivery cart, or pulled her hand from an attacking paper shredder, how could an office manager save someone's life at work?* Bill wondered. "How did he do that? He's good, but how do you save someone's life in an office?"

Sylvia laughed. "As you probably already know, when Peter became our V.P., this department was a mess. We hated our jobs and each other," she began.

"It was a typical Crystal-Display department," Bill smiled knowingly.

"Peter felt the only way to turn the department around was to change the direction of the staff. He started doing things to help us be more successful—develop our skills, improve communication, and make work a more pleasant place to be.

"One of the new programs he started was a series of what he

called, 'Success Seminars.' These sessions taught us how to relate better to ourselves and to others. Peter felt that if we were healthier emotionally, we would be more productive and successful at work."

"How did people accept the seminars?" Bill asked.

"At first we were skeptical, critical, and cynical of course. That's the way we were about everything related to work. But the seminars were mandatory and were held during work hours, so even the most cynical person was happy to get off work for an hour. The presenters were very practical, helpful, and funny. People quickly warmed up to the events and started to enjoy them. They taught us how to look inside ourselves, recognize problems, and begin to do something about them. I figured I was okay, but I *knew* there were many people present who needed help," she winked again and smiled at Bill.

"One of the seminars was about depression at work. A doctor came and told us that depression is a serious problem in the workplace. I had no idea that up to six percent of employees have a mood disorder like depression, anxiety, or mood swings. He said it often starts in their teen years and gradually worsens, so it affects people in their prime working years. I was surprised when he said that only twenty percent of people who have depression will ever be diagnosed or treated. The rest just stay at work and ignore the problem as it slowly worsens their performance, judgment, energy, concentration, productivity, creativity, and relationships. That sure described a lot of people in our department. I was hoping they were hearing the message and preparing to get help.

"The doctor said that untreated depression is costing our national economy billions of dollars due to lost productivity, absenteeism, employee turnover and treatment costs. He said that more than half of disability claims are related to mental health problems. The doctor emphasized that with early diagnosis and treatment, disability rates drop, productivity increases, and corporations can save millions of dollars. He even told us how to diagnose depression so we could check ourselves."

"Wow, how do you do that?" asked Bill.

"It's really not that difficult. We were told to watch for worsening concentration, lack of interest in things, social isolation, low energy, irritability, not being able to shut your mind off, and a bunch of other things. He described most of our department," Sylvia said with a grin.

"He suggested that everyone who was feeling this way should see a doctor and get treated so they would be able to function better now and avoid disability later. He really encouraged the supervisors to understand this condition so they could help their staff get treated early."

"That's an unusual topic for a work seminar," Bill commented.

"Yes, you're right, but it was just like Peter to do something like that. He was very innovative and would do whatever helped the staff be happier and more productive. He created a *culture of recovery*, so everyone could be honest about themselves and their work. This helped us pull together and assist each other.'"

"Did the seminar help you?"

"Not at first. I thought it was just interesting information. There were lots of others I knew who really needed it. I had often had down times in my life but I was still able to function at work, so I didn't think I had a problem.

"Over the next year, however, my life really took a bad turn. My husband lost his job and my best friend was diagnosed with cancer. There were just a whole lot of difficult circumstances that just seemed to pile up and get overwhelming. I started to worry too much. First about money, since my husband was stuck at home, then about the kids getting sick, then about having car accidents; I just couldn't shut it off. I became preoccupied with worry even at work. I became pessimistic about everything since so many things seemed to be going wrong. I decided to avoid talking to people because they would just upset me or I may upset them. I ate lunch alone and avoided meetings and conversations. At work I just couldn't shut my mind off from all this negative thinking. It was like I was listening to a continuous audio tape of negative thoughts."

"So what did you do about it?"

"Nothing of course. I thought I was fine—just a bit stressed out with life's circumstances. I could still do my job, though more slowly and with a great deal more effort. Since I was functioning, I thought I didn't need help. I was a strong person, so I figured I could handle it myself.

"One morning at work I was feeling really stressed. I hadn't slept all night because I was so worried about my kids who were away visiting relatives. When I opened my day schedule, I realized to my horror that I had forgotten to complete a report that I had promised Peter to have ready that day. It had totally slipped my mind. I felt like such an incompetent, unreliable loser. I had never missed anything like that before. I just dissolved into a pile of tears and put my head down on my desk feeling completely defeated. My mind filled with tormenting thoughts like, Everyone would be better off without me! I am a liability to the company and the family. Just end it all now. Death is the only way to stop the pain.

"As you might guess, that's when Peter walked past my desk and saw the state I was in. Without any words, and without attracting attention, he motioned me into his office. I was sure he would fire me. I felt so hopeless. Then, when I was in his office with the door closed, he said something amazing. He said, 'Is there anything I can do to help?'

"I just burst into tears and told him everything that was going wrong in my life. When I was done, Peter paused for a moment and said, 'Do you remember the seminar we had with the doctor?'

"'Sure,' I said. 'I was there.'

"He asked me, 'Do you think you might be depressed?'

"That just sent me into another volley of tears. I didn't need yet another problem to deal with. I believed I was too strong to be depressed. Depression was just for weak people who couldn't pull themselves together.

"Then he reminded me of our seminar with the doctor. He asked me if I remembered the checklist of symptoms of depression he gave us so we could diagnose ourselves. He had it handy. He asked me, 'Do you think we could do it together?'

"I just kind of nodded weakly. I was totally ashamed to be going through this in Peter's office. Then he asked me the questions.

"'Do you notice that you can't shut your mind off?'

"'Yes'

"'Are those thoughts mostly negative with sadness, worry, pessimism?'

"I nodded.

"'Do you feel like a failure, that everything is your fault?'

"Of course I did. I told him I'd made a mess of everything!

"'Is it getting harder to concentrate?'

"I couldn't concentrate.

"'Is it hard to shut your mind off to sleep?'

"It had been impossible. I couldn't stop worrying.

"'Have your energy and ambition disappeared so you are always tired and find life to be just a big struggle?'

"I nodded again. *Wow*, I thought, *how can he be reading my mind so accurately*?

"'Are you avoiding people and prefer to be alone?'

"I didn't want to bother people with my problems.

"'Do you feel that life is not worth living and that you would be better off…dead?'

"That was too much. I dissolved into tears again with that question.

"Peter waited. He just looked at me in a very caring and sympathetic way. Then he asked, 'Do you have a plan to end your life?'

"I told him no, I did not. Not at that point. I didn't want to die, I just wanted the pain to stop. I wanted to wave a magic wand so all the problems would go away.

"Then he posed the question. 'So what do you think? Would depression be a possibility?'

"He was being gentle with me, but there was no doubt in my mind that I had most of the symptoms on the list. I had to agree that I was depressed. But Peter didn't stop there. 'So what are you going to do to solve this problem?' he asked.

"I told him I'd have to go see a doctor.

"He handed me the phone so I would make the appointment before I left his office. With the appointment made, he told me to go home and return when my doctor said I was ready to come back to work."

"What a meeting!" Bill said realizing the significance of this event for Sylvia.

"What a guy, that Peter! Sylvia echoed. He knew just what to do and he started me on my recovery journey. He really did save my life. I don't know what might have happened if he hadn't helped me that day."

"So what happened after that?"

"My doctor agreed that I was depressed and started me on an antidepressant to increase my brain serotonin levels. The first one made me sick and groggy, so I had to try a few before I found the right one. Over the next two months I slowly improved. My mind cleared, my energy improved, and I could concentrate again. When my doctor felt I was well enough, I returned to work but on a gradual basis. I started just part time and slowly increased my hours.

"On my first day back I felt quite embarrassed that I had been off because of a mental problem. I tried to avoid as many people as possible. A funny thing happened that day, though. At least three people came up to me privately and told me that they too had started antidepressants since the depression seminar and were feeling so much better. I realized what a common and well concealed condition depression was.

"A few months after I'd come back to work and things were going well, Peter called me into his office. I brought him up to date on how well I was feeling, but he raised a new issue that really surprised me. He asked me if I'd noticed that I was carrying a bag.

"My first response was, 'What bag?' and then I kind of realized what he was talking about. 'Oh, that bag,' I said. 'Sure, I've noticed it but it's no big deal. I can manage fine with it.' I asked him why he wanted to know.

"He just said, 'You need to get rid of it, trust me.'

"I wondered why he was so adamant. He acted as if he knew what was in it, so I asked him.

"'It's the story of your life,' he told me. 'It contains every painful memory and every lie that you have believed about yourself. As long as you carry it around, it shapes your attitudes about yourself and others. It colors your relationships and greatly limits your success potential.'

"I definitely didn't want something like that hanging off me. 'How do I get rid of it?' I asked.

"He handed me a business card and said it was the name of the person who helped him get rid of his bag. 'She's a counselor,' he said, 'and an expert in baggage. Go talk to her and see what happens.'

"So I did. It was an amazing experience. She helped me go through the bag and recognize all the painful events of my past that caused me to believe lies about myself and others. I was then able to see how my expectations, attitudes, and relationships had all been shaped by past hurts and the resulting lies. The counselor helped me deal with all the memories and tear up all the lies. It was so liberating! I felt so much freer and stronger when it was all over.

"A couple of months later Peter called me into his office once again. I was really touched by his genuine interest in me. He asked me how things were going.

"'Really well,' I told him. I'd actually never felt that well. I'd stopped worrying so much, I could concentrate, and I felt much more confident. Getting along with people and working with them was so much easier now.

"He was very pleased with my progress. He said he had seen real change in me over that past year. 'Where's your bag?' he joked with me.

"'Gone forever!' I was so proud to tell him that. He had really been right about the value of that counselor.

"'So—I have an important question for you,' he said. 'Would you consider becoming a supervisor?'

"Wow! What a question! I was shocked and excited at the same time. I had never considered myself to be management material, but I knew that was because of some lies from my former bag.

"'Why me?' I asked him.

"'Because you have overcome significant personal obstacles and as a result you understand and have a heart for people. You're authentic. You don't live behind a mask. You're an excellent worker and can be trusted.' Then he said it was most of all because I had had the courage to face depression and my bag and get rid of them both. He told me that's why I'd make a good leader. I wouldn't be limited by the lies I had once believed about myself. He said he had asked others to deal with their bags but they refused, and on that basis they would never qualify for promotion.

"It didn't take me long to answer. 'Okay,' I said. 'If you think I can do it, then I will.'

"So, I've been a supervisor here ever since and I've never been happier or more satisfied. I've been able to help some of my staff get rid of their bags, too. I'm preparing them for promotions."

"What a wonderful story!" Bill concluded, but he wasn't a bit surprised by it anymore. He knew Peter, and he had confidence in what Peter could do. He closed his notebook thoughtfully. These past few conversations had instilled in him genuine hope. He also had all the information he needed to finish his report and to make recommendations to Globalcorp. But what he had to say would likely be unorthodox. He smiled at Sylvia. "Thank you so much for sharing something so personal with me." They both rose to their feet, and Bill extended a hand. "It's very clear to me now what makes this department so different."

Back in his usual spot in the cafeteria, Bill wrote down his observations:

Depression is a serious problem in the workplace. It results in days lost during disability, lost productivity, and poor relationships among those who continue to work while depressed.

Something as simple as a depression seminar can remove the stigma of mental illness, get people into treatment earlier, reduce disability days, and even save lives.

Supervisors can make a big difference in helping depressed workers get help early.

Those who are willing to face their emotional baggage and get rid of it make the best leaders and role models.

Leadership development requires healthy emotions.

People skills improve as baggage is removed.

Departments are more productive and pleasant places to work as staff get rid of their bags.

The Report

When Bill returned to his hotel room that evening, three urgent messages from Len Maxwell awaited him. Mr. B. had called an emergency meeting to discuss the restructuring of Crystal-Display. Len needed Bill's report right away. The pressure was on!

Bill hit the delete key and answered mentally. *Don't worry, Len. The report's on the way. I'll cancel all the remaining interviews and get writing.*

Bill settled on the couch and pulled out his notebook to review his key observations.

"So how do I summarize all that?" he asked out loud. "I can't send a report about 'bags'; they'll think I'm nuts. I just won't mention them."

Several things are very clear, Bill keyed into his laptop. *Crystal-Display has a product that is in demand. It should be profitable. The company, however, has a* people *problem, which has created performance, quality, and service issues. This has led to loss of market share, smaller margins and dismal financial performance.*

The leadership is paralyzed, dysfunctional, inefficient, and immature. They set the standard with their behavior, and model dysfunction for the entire company. As long as this people problem is not addressed, there is no hope for the company to recover.

However, there is one departmental anomaly, Bill continued. *The Communications department. The vice president of this department has resolved his own issues and as a result is leading a department that has the best financial performance in the company. He models a balanced personality with a healthy respect and interest in others. Not only is his department reaching all their productivity goals, but he is training a leadership team and teaching them how to develop healthy attitudes. If this pattern can be repeated in all the other departments, then I predict a financial turnaround for the entire company within three years.*

How did this V.P. achieve these financial and staff results? His strategy looks like this:

He has created a culture of recovery. *His leadership philosophy is built on the premise that everyone has struggles of some kind, but that all should be progressing toward a goal of improvement. The V.P. is as comfortable discussing recovery issues as company issues, primarily because of his own recovery journey. Promotions come to those who demonstrate leadership ability and emotional well being.*

Staff are encouraged to see a counselor whenever they find themselves struggling. The V.P. models this strategy and encourages it. He makes it clear that resolving past hurts with a counselor is key to moving forward both at work and at home.

He also encourages healthy, active, personal spirituality. He describes it as a basis for integrity, as a foundation for meaning in life and in work, and as a source of inner strength for coping with major stress, and for initiating significant behavioral changes.

This department offers regular mental health seminars to help people recognize depression and other common mood disorders. Awareness of symptoms makes it possible for them to seek the medical help they require early in the course of the illness, and in some cases even before they become disabled by it.

Because of these steps, this department has a friendly, mutually helpful, and very productive working environment. Staff attitudes are markedly different from those within the rest of the company. I believe this difference in attitude is the key to their outstanding performance numbers.

In summary, this is a failing company that conventional wisdom would say should be sold or closed as soon as possible. I, however, feel that the company might be saved if the principles demonstrated in the Communications department are implemented throughout Crystal-Display. There is significant demand for their product, so I believe financial performance will improve quickly with the right management in place.

To implement this recommendation, the entire existing senior management needs to be replaced. I recommend that Peter Wilson, the vice president of Communications, be considered as the new CEO and be allowed to choose the senior management team from among the leaders he has been training. He could then implement the same recovery strategy throughout the company that he is using so successfully in the Communications department.

I would also like to add, on a personal note, that if these recom-

mendations are accepted, I would be willing to assist the new CEO in the implementation of this aggressive strategy.

Bill was satisfied both with his investigation, and with his report. *I've never written a report quite like this before,* he smiled to himself imagining Len Maxwell's face as he read it. He hit "send." *I hope Len can handle it.*

The Decision

The heat was really on, and Len Maxwell was feeling it. The vice presidents would be meeting with Mr. B. that afternoon. Len was scheduled to present the report and recommendations on Crystal-Display to the group. His job was clearly on the line, and the wait for Bill Spencer's report had been unbearable. He trusted Bill's judgment, however, and was very relieved to have received the report the previous night.

Bill was right. Len paced his office floor, report in hand. He certainly found it to be very unusual. Instead of being filled with performance data and balance sheets, this report was all about people, emotions, and leadership.

Len was concerned. *How will Mr. B. and the other V.P.'s respond to a report that stresses the "soft" side of business?* His anxious mind grappled with a variety of thoughts. *Will they take this report seriously or just laugh me out of the room? No—I have to trust Bill. He has rescued or dispatched many floundering Globalcorp companies in the past and is greatly respected for his shrewd analyses.*

There was no time left to change the report or send it back to Bill for reworking. Len decided to accept it and present it enthusiastically, even though he really wasn't sure what Bill was talking about.

In the boardroom that afternoon, the time came to discuss Crystal-Display. Mr. B. turned to Len and barked, "Maxwell, what's the story on Crystal-Display?"

With all the artificial courage he could muster, Len stepped to the front of the room and presented Bill's entire report along with the recommendations. He then waited for a response.

There was none. There was nothing but a very long, uncomfortable silence.

Len could feel the blade of the guillotine rising above his head. He was right. They had never heard a report like that before. No one had ever raised the issue of there being emotionally dysfunctional people at management level, nor had anyone ever mentioned the destructive effects dysfunctional managers could have on the corporate bottom line.

He didn't know that the vice presidents in the room, and even Mr. B. himself, were feeling convicted of the possibility that they themselves may be suffering from similar problems. A self-conscious awkwardness hung in the room as they came to terms with their weaknesses. Everyone but Mr. B. studied their notes and wished they could melt into the floor. Len's heart was pounding, his knees were shaking, and he felt lightheaded as he stood waiting.

"*Bill* wrote all that?" Mr. B.'s voice suddenly cracked the silence.

"Yes, sir, every word," Len steadied himself against the boardroom table. His mouth was dry and he had to clear his throat several times just to form those few words.

There was another long silence as they were forced to either question the judgment of their most trusted troubleshooter or accept his recommendations.

"Then do it!" Mr. B's voice didn't carry quite the same bravado, although his resolve remained intact. "You have sixty days to initiate everything Bill suggested. Now get out of here and start making phone calls."

Len couldn't get out of there fast enough. He raced to his office, loosened his tie, collapsed in his chair, and waited for his pulse to slow down. He had escaped the axe. Bill's reputation saved him. He owed Bill lunch. No, dinner. No, perhaps a new house. Fingers still trembling, Len started flipping through the company phone directory for phone numbers, but he was interrupted by a knock on the door.

"Come in," he called out.

It was Senior Vice President Charlotte Edwards. Len was stunned. She never came to his office or associated with junior vice presidents. Was the axe going to fall now?

Edwards closed the door behind herself and floated to a chair facing his desk. "That was a very unusual report," she began.

"Yes, I was quite surprised myself, but it did make sense," Len answered, feigning familiarity with the topic.

"Yes," Charlotte agreed, "It really got me thinking... about our Head Office here. Do you think we might have some of the same problems?"

Len didn't know how to handle this explosive question. His

primary goal as the most junior vice president was to stay out of trouble and not upset anyone.

"Well," he paused. He pretended to be thoughtfully analyzing the situation. Really he was struggling to find a diplomatic answer. "Perhaps there is room for improvement." Momentary relief flooded him. He was very proud that he had come up with such a safe response.

"I think we do," Charlotte continued, "and you seem to have a breakthrough solution along with a good understanding of these issues."

Len almost choked when he realized that she thought he understood Bill's report.

"I want to initiate those same changes here at Globalcorp that you are going to start at Crystal-Display. If you are going to head up the process there, could you also direct the transitions here?"

Len didn't know if he should laugh or cry. A few hours ago he thought he was going to be fired for presenting such a weak report. Now he was considered the Head Office expert in corporate emotional transformation.

"Why certainly, I'd be glad to," Len managed a confident tone he had learned in high school drama class.

Charlotte rose to leave. "Good," she said. "Let me know when the seminar series begins, so I can be at every one."

When the door closed behind her, Len wilted in his chair. He exhaled as if he had been holding his breath the whole time and his arms fell loosely to his sides. He suddenly felt very tired. "What happened to me these past few hours?" he wondered aloud. It seemed as if life had shot past him and he was running hard to catch up. *It will be hard enough to turn Crystal-Display around, but now I have to change Globalcorp, too? What have I gotten into? I don't even know what the heck Bill is talking about.* He made a quick decision. *I need Peter Wilson. I need to call him right now to set up a meeting.* He found Peter's number, dialed it, and stood to his feet, pacing impatiently as the call went through.

When he finally had Peter on the line, he took a step back to sit down in his chair, "Hello. This is Len Maxwell, your new regional vice pres ... Ow!"

A sharp pain shot through his leg as he fell against his desk. It was all he could do to regain his balance. "What in the world?"

He heard Peter's concern on the other end. "Are you all right?"

"Oh, sorry Peter. I don't know! I just tripped over something. A bag? It's a ... large bag I've never seen before, and it's ... attached to my wrist?"

"Oh! I think I can help," Peter replied. "When can we meet?"

Endnotes

1. She was misinterpreting *Fish: A Remarkable Way to Boost Morale and Improve Results* by Lundin, Paul and Christensen.
2. He was misinterpreting *The One Minute Manager* by Kenneth Blanchard.
3. He was misinterpreting *Who Moved My Cheese* by Spencer Johnson.
4. He was misinterpreting *The Innovator's Dilemma* by Clayton Christensen.